Happy Bi
michael
from joannie
+
Russell (the boy)

Join Anno for a wonderful adventure of the imagination into the realm of people and places. With the artist as your guide, you'll meet a fascinating variety of children and adults busy at work and at play, on farms, in villages, or in towns and cities. You'll also recognize familiar characters from favorite tales, and see new stories without words unfold from page to page, in the tradition of Japanese scroll painting.

The characteristic art and architecture of northern Europe are pictured in meticulously rendered watercolors, and references to great European composers are skillfully included. But look carefully! For, as in all of Mitsumasa Anno's books, keen-eyed viewers can also find visual jokes and puzzles, as well as tricks of perspective in space and time.

Mitsumasa Anno is known all around the world for his beautiful and imaginative picture books, designed for children, but appreciated and enjoyed by adults as well. Anno's record in this book of his recent travels through northern Europe is a *tour de force* of variety and continuity, highly personal, yet also following in the tradition of such famous Japanese artists as the 8th century envoy to China, Kibi, and the Zen Buddhist painter, Sesshu Toyo (1420–1506). Kibi's scroll painting is crowded with people and adventures, stories told in picture form. Sesshu painted a 50-foot long handscroll, a continuously evolving sequence of landscape motifs and changing seasons, which helped to formulate both his art style and his philosophy. Like them, Anno, too, was discovering some of his artistic and philosophic "roots" as he travelled and observed.

In this book, Mitsumasa Anno shows once again his genius for depicting reality as seen through the inventive eye of the artist, and thus he extends the imagination and creativity of all those who travel with him.

Anno's Journey was the winner of *The Boston Globe/Horn Book* Award in 1978, as well as an American Library Association Notable Children's Book.

Anno's Journey
MITSUMASA ANNO

PHILOMEL BOOKS

OTHER BOOKS BY
MITSUMASA ANNO

Anno's Alphabet
Anno's Animals
Anno's Britain
Anno's Counting Book
Anno's Counting House
Anno's Italy
Anno's Magical ABC:
An Anamorphic Alphabet
Anno's Medieval World
The King's Flower
The Unique World of Mitsumasa Anno:
Selected Works (1968–1977)

Library of Congress Cataloging in Publication Data
Anno, Mitsumasa, 1926-   Anno's journey.
SUMMARY: Records in drawings the author's journey through northern Europe and his impressions of the land,
the people at work and play, and their art, architecture, folklore, and fairy tales.
[1. Europe—Pictorial works. 2. Stories without words] I. Title.
PZ7.A5875Ar 1978   [E]   77-16336
ISBN 0-399-20762-7
ISBN 0-399-20952-2 paperback
Fourth printing 1982.
Published by Philomel Books, The Putnam Publishing Group, 51 Madison Ave., New York, N.Y. 10010.
Originally published in the U.S.A. by William Collins Publishers, Inc., 1978.
Copyright © 1977 by Fukuinkan Shoten Publishers, Tokyo. Japanese edition entitled MY JOURNEY.
All rights reserved. Printed in the United States of America.

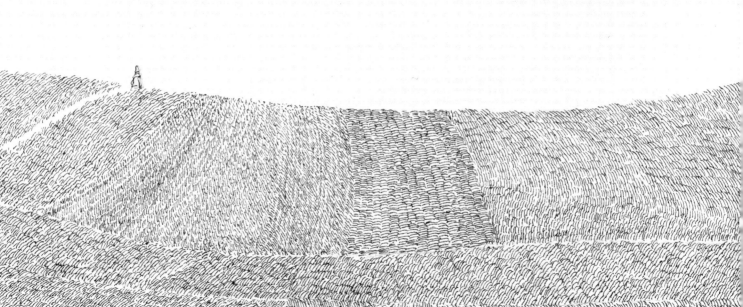

Since childhood Mitsumasa Anno has been fascinated by Europe, by its varied landscape, its art and architecture, its folklore and fairy tale, its people at their work and play. In 1963 and again in 1975 Anno left his native Japan and journeyed through many parts of Europe exploring, observing, painting and drawing as he went. He found a world new to him, as it will be to many of his readers, but a world that is deeply rooted in ancient traditions. This book is a record of that journey. Go with the lone traveller on his way and you will encounter the paintings of the French Impressionists, find musical notes from Beethoven's Ninth, tilt at the windmill with Don Quixote and Sancho Panza, help to pull up The Big Enormous Turnip. Every double-page spread in this book contains a whole host of friends for those who can find them, and each traveller with Anno can create his own version of the story. Mitsumasa Anno writes of his journey: 'I followed the path wherever it went, up and down hills, across rivers, through fields which spread out into great open spaces. There were forests and rivers wherever I travelled; in the forests there were deer and in the rivers there were trout. At the end of the road there were always houses gathered together to make a town, and in every town there were gates, leading from shops to squares and plazas, through graveyards and gardens to churches and cathedrals. One town had a castle in its midst; one castle was a town by itself. They gave me an image of the country, and each reflected the life of that town, that country.

'I wandered from town to town, from country to country and sometimes my journey was hard, but it is at just such times that the reward comes. When a man loses his way, he often finds himself—or some unlooked-for treasure. By the end of my journey, I realized that I had set out not to collect information but to lose my way—and to discover the world you will find in this book.

'It is a world filled with variety, yet a simple place with a deep-rooted sense of culture, an appreciation of nature that preserves it from destruction and pollution. It is a beautiful world.'

Here are some things to look for in *Anno's Journey*:

Details from paintings by Courbet, Millet, Renoir, Seurat and others; all sorts of children's games; an escaping prisoner; some characters from *Sesame Street*, from *The Pied Piper of Hamelin*, *The Emperor's New Clothes*, *Red Riding Hood*, *Pinocchio*, *Don Quixote* and other beloved stories; a romantic tale, continued on several pages, of love and retribution; a race; Beethoven sitting at a window; an emptying bottle on a shop sign, to mention just a few.

The Tale of Peter Rabbit

by Beatrix Potter • illustrated by Amye Rosenberg

A GOLDEN BOOK • NEW YORK

Western Publishing Company, Inc., Racine, Wisconsin 53404

nce upon a time there were four little rabbits, and their names were:

Flopsy   Mopsy   Cottontail   and Peter

They lived with their mother in a sandbank, underneath the root of a very big fir tree.

"Now, my dears," said old Mrs. Rabbit one morning, "you may go into the fields or down the lane, but don't go into Mr. McGregor's garden. Your father had an accident there; he was put into a pie by Mrs. McGregor. Now run along, and don't get into mischief. I am going out."

Then old Mrs. Rabbit took a basket and her umbrella and went through the wood to the baker's. She bought a loaf of brown bread and five currant buns.

Flopsy, Mopsy, and Cottontail, who were good little bunnies, went down the lane to gather blackberries.

But Peter, who was very naughty, ran straight away to Mr. McGregor's garden and squeezed under the gate!

First he ate some lettuce
and some French beans, and
then he ate some radishes.
And then, feeling rather sick,
he went to look for some parsley.

But round the end of a cucumber frame, whom should he meet but Mr. McGregor!

Mr. McGregor was on his hands and knees planting out young cabbages, but he jumped up and ran after Peter, waving a rake and calling out, "Stop, thief!"

Peter was most dreadfully frightened. He rushed all over the garden, for he had forgotten the way back to the gate. He lost one of his shoes among the cabbages, and the other shoe amongst the potatoes.

After losing them, he ran on four legs and went faster, so that I think he might have got away altogether if he had not unfortunately run into a gooseberry net and got caught by the large buttons on his jacket. It was a blue jacket with brass buttons, quite new.

Peter gave himself up for lost and shed big tears. But his sobs were overheard by some friendly sparrows, who flew to him in great excitement and implored him to exert himself.

Mr. McGregor came up with a sieve which he intended
to pop upon the top of Peter. But Peter wriggled out just
in time, leaving his jacket behind him . . .

and rushed into the toolshed
and jumped into a can.

It would have been a beautiful
thing to hide in, if it had not
had so much water in it.

Mr. McGregor was quite sure that Peter was somewhere
in the toolshed, perhaps hidden underneath a flowerpot.
He began to turn them over carefully, looking under each.
Presently Peter sneezed—*Kertyschoo!*

Mr. McGregor was after him in no time and tried to put his foot upon Peter, who jumped out of a window, upsetting three plants. The window was too small for Mr. McGregor, and he was tired of running after Peter. He went back to his work.

Peter sat down to rest. He was out of breath and trembling with fright, and he had not the least idea which way to go.

After a time he began to wander about—going lippity, lippity, not very fast, and looking around.

He found a door in a wall, but it was locked, and there was no room for a fat little rabbit to squeeze underneath.

An old mouse was running in and out over the stone
doorstep, carrying peas and beans to her family in the
wood. Peter asked her the way to the gate, but she had
such a large pea in her mouth that she could not answer.
She only shook her head at him. Peter began to cry.

Then he tried to find his way straight across the garden, but he became more and more puzzled. Presently, he came to a pond where Mr. McGregor filled his watering cans. A white cat was staring at some goldfish; she sat very, very still. But now and then the tip of her tail twitched as if it were alive. Peter thought it best to go away without speaking to her; he had heard about cats from his cousin, little Benjamin Bunny.

He went back towards the toolshed, but suddenly,
quite close to him, he heard the noise of a hoe—
scr-r-ritch, scratch, scratch, scritch.

Peter scuttered underneath the bushes. But presently, as nothing happened, he came out and climbed upon a wheelbarrow and peeped over. The first thing he saw was Mr. McGregor hoeing onions. His back was turned towards Peter, and beyond him was the gate!

Peter got down very quietly off the wheelbarrow and
started running as fast as he could go along a straight walk
behind some black-currant bushes. Mr. McGregor caught
sight of him at the corner....

But Peter did not care. He slipped underneath the gate and was safe at last in the wood outside the garden.

Mr. McGregor hung up the little jacket and the shoes for a scarecrow to frighten the blackbirds.

Peter never stopped running or looked behind him till he got home to the big fir tree. He was so tired that he flopped down upon the nice soft sand on the floor of the rabbit hole and shut his eyes. His mother was busy cooking; she wondered what he had done with his clothes. It was the second little jacket and pair of shoes that Peter had lost in a fortnight!

I am sorry to say that Peter was not very well during
the evening. His mother put him to bed and made some
camomile tea, and she gave a dose of it to Peter!
"One tablespoonful to be taken at bedtime."
But Flopsy, Mopsy, and Cottontail had bread and milk
and blackberries for supper.